Team Spirit

THE HOUSTON ROCKETS

BY

MARK STEWART

Content Consultant
Matt Zeysing
Historian and Archivist
The Naismith Memorial Basketball Hall of Fame

NORWOOD HOUSE PRESS

CHICAGO, ILLINOIS

Norwood House Press
P.O. Box 316598
Chicago, Illinois 60631

For information regarding Norwood House Press, please visit our website at:
www.norwoodhousepress.com or call 866-565-2900.

All photos courtesy of Getty Images except the following:
Black Book Partners Archives (6, 34),
Topps, Inc. (7, 14, 20, 21, 29, 35 top right, 37, 38, 40 bottom left, 43),
The Star Company (35 top left, 40 top left), Houston Rockets (41 top)
Matt Richman (48).
Cover image: Sam Forencich/Getty Images
Special thanks to Topps, Inc.

Editor: Mike Kennedy
Designer: Ron Jaffe
Project Management: Black Book Partners, LLC.
Research: Joshua Zaffos

Special thanks to Victoria and Alexandra Rosch and Marc Vandermeer

Library of Congress Cataloging-in-Publication Data

Stewart, Mark, 1960-
  The Houston Rockets / by Mark Stewart ; content consultant, Matt
Zeysing.
    p. cm. -- (Team spirit)
  Includes bibliographical references and index.
  Summary: "Presents the history and accomplishments of the Houston
Rockets basketball team. Includes highlights of players, coaches, and awards,
quotes, timelines, maps, glossary and websites"--Provided by publisher.
  ISBN-13: 978-1-59953-283-7 (library edition : alk. paper)
  ISBN-10: 1-59953-283-2 (library edition : alk. paper) 1. Houston Rockets
(Basketball team)--History--Juvenile literature. 2.
Basketball--Texas--Houston--History--Juvenile literature. I. Zeysing, Matt.
II. Title.
  GV885.52.H65S74 2009
  796.323'64097641411--dc22
                                              2008044306

COVER PHOTO: The Rockets celebrate a win during the 2007–08 season.

Table of Contents

CHAPTER	PAGE
Meet the Rockets	4
Way Back When	6
The Team Today	10
Home Court	12
Dressed For Success	14
We Won!	16
Go-To Guys	20
On the Sidelines	24
One Great Day	26
Legend Has It	28
It Really Happened	30
Team Spirit	32
Timeline	34
Fun Facts	36
Talking Hoops	38
For the Record	40
Pinpoints	42
Play Ball	44
Glossary	46
Places to Go	47
Index	48

SPORTS WORDS & VOCABULARY WORDS: In this book, you will find many words that are new to you. You may also see familiar words used in new ways. The glossary on page 46 gives the meanings of basketball words, as well as "everyday" words that have special basketball meanings. These words appear in **bold type** throughout the book. The glossary on page 47 gives the meanings of vocabulary words that are not related to basketball. They appear in ***bold italic type*** throughout the book.

BASKETBALL SEASONS: Because each basketball season begins late in one year and ends early in the next, seasons are not named after years. Instead, they are written out as two years separated by a dash, for example 1944–45 or 2005–06.

Meet the Rockets

It takes skill, toughness, and teamwork to win games in the **National Basketball Association (NBA)**. The size of a player does not always matter. The size of his heart is more important. When it comes to playing for a championship, however, a team must have something else: a superstar center. It is almost impossible to win without one.

Fans of the Houston Rockets know this better than anyone. The Rockets have reached the **NBA Finals** four times. Each time they had the NBA's best "big man"—and a great cast of stars and **substitutes** surrounding him. That has always been a *formula* for success in Houston.

This book tells the story of the Rockets. They have had many wonderful players over the years. They have recorded many famous victories. And when the Rockets have had that special man in the middle, they have been true *contenders* for the NBA title.

Shane Battier and Yao Ming soar high for a rebound during a 2007–08 game.

Way Back When

T he Rockets were born during a basketball "war" between the NBA and the new **American Basketball Association (ABA)**. In 1967, the ABA began play with teams in 11 cities. Two of those clubs were on the West Coast, where the NBA also had a pair of teams. To stay ahead of the ABA, the NBA added two more clubs, the San Diego Rockets and the Seattle Supersonics. Both teams were made up of unwanted players from other NBA clubs.

In their first year, the Rockets were led by three forwards—John

Block, Don Kojis, and Dave Gambee. Their top **draft pick** in 1967 was Pat Riley. He later became a great NBA coach. Riley played only three years with the Rockets.

The team had more luck in the 1968 draft. After winning a coin flip with the Baltimore Bullets, the Rockets were awarded the first pick. They chose Elvin Hayes. The high-scoring forward guided the Rockets to the **playoffs** as a **rookie**. Hayes was the NBA's scoring champion in his first season and the league's top rebounder in his second season.

In 1971, a group of *investors* from Texas bought the Rockets and moved them to Houston. By the mid-1970s, the team featured a new group of talented, hardworking players that included Calvin Murphy, Rudy Tomjanovich, and Mike Newlin. When the ABA went out of business in 1976, the Rockets made a trade for 21-year-old Moses Malone. He had been the best young center in the *defunct* league. Malone led the Rockets to the top of the **Central Division** for the first time.

In 1980–81, Malone, Murphy, and Tomjanovich were the heart of the team that reached the NBA Finals. Malone piled up more than 2,000 points and 1,000 rebounds. A year later, he was named the league's **Most Valuable Player (MVP)**. The Rockets returned to the NBA Finals in 1986. The stars of that team were Hakeem Olajuwon and Ralph Sampson, a pair of *agile* centers who could score and block shots. Unfortunately, in both years, Houston lost the NBA Championship to the Boston Celtics.

The team's first championship came in 1993–94. Olajuwon was still at the top of his game. He was joined by a group of excellent **role players**, including guards Sam Cassell, Kenny Smith, and

LEFT: Elvin Hayes, the team's first great star.
ABOVE: Moses Malone, who led the Rockets to the NBA Finals in 1981.

Vernon Maxwell, and forwards Robert Horry and Otis Thorpe. Tomjanovich, Houston's former star, coached the team to victory over the New York Knicks in the NBA Finals.

One year later, the Rockets returned to the top of **professional** basketball. Olajuwon's old college teammate Clyde Drexler came to Houston in the middle of the season. The two superstars led the Rockets past Shaquille O'Neal and the Orlando Magic in the NBA Finals.

Later in the 1990s, the Rockets added Charles Barkley to their **lineup** of stars. Houston looked like it was on its way to the NBA Finals again in 1996–97, but the team lost to the Utah Jazz in the **Western Conference Finals**. In the years that followed, age and injuries ended Houston's great run. As the 21st *century* began, the team started to rebuild with new players. As always, their star search focused on finding a great center.

LEFT: Hakeem Olajuwon shoots a jump shot. He led Houston to the NBA Championship twice. **ABOVE**: Clyde Drexler, who teamed with Olajuwon for the team's second title.

9

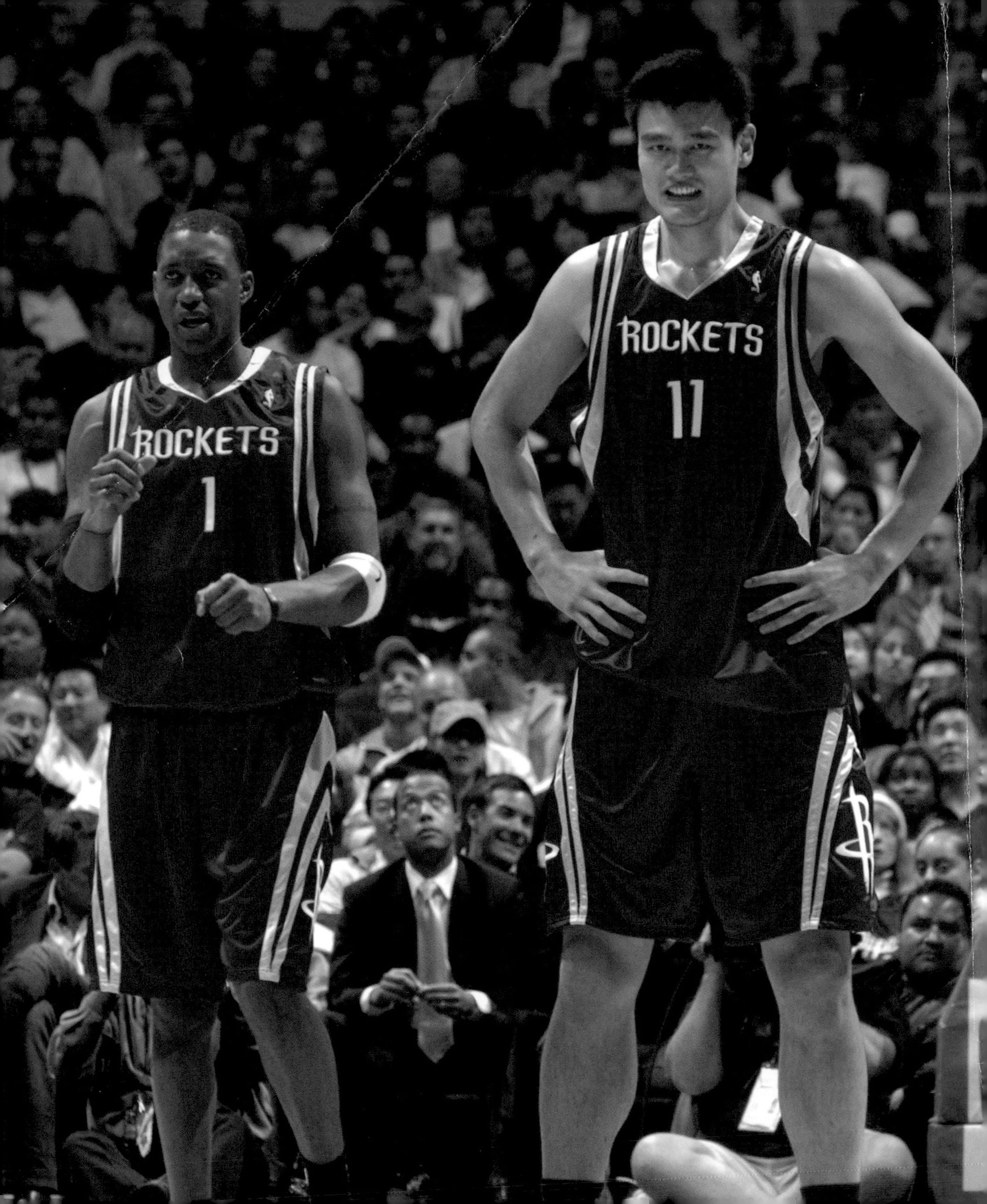
ROCKETS
1
ROCKETS
11

The Team Today

In 2002, the Rockets blasted off when they chose Yao Ming with the first pick in the **NBA draft**. Yao was from China. He stood taller than seven feet, but he had the smooth moves of a much smaller player. He also had a warm personality and a sharp sense of humor. Soon the Rockets were playing winning basketball again.

As Yao found his way in the NBA, the Rockets looked for players who would work well with him. In 2004, Tracy McGrady joined the team. Building on the talents of these two stars, Houston took aim at a return to the NBA Finals.

In 2007–08, Yao and McGrady were working well together and finding ways to make their teammates better. Unfortunately, Yao broke his foot. Some fans gave up hope. But the Rockets did not. They continued winning without their great center. At one point, Houston won 22 games in a row—the second-longest winning streak in NBA history. Although the Rockets fell short of the league title, they proved to themselves and the rest of the league that they were a team in every sense of the word.

Tracy McGrady and Yao Ming get ready to dig in on defense during the 2007–08 season.

Home Court

After moving from San Diego to Houston, the Rockets had to await several years before they settled into one arena. They played their home games in cities all over Texas, including Houston, San Antonio, and Waco. Sometimes, they had to host games out of the state. They played in Albuquerque, New Mexico—and even a few games back in San Diego!

Finally, in 1975, the Rockets opened a new arena called the Summit. They shared it with a hockey team known as the Aeros. The Rockets were tough to beat in the Summit when it was filled with screaming fans.

In 2002, the city began building a new arena in downtown Houston. The Rockets moved into it at the start of the 2003–04 season. Their new arena is roomy and modern. It is also a great place to see music concerts.

BY THE NUMBERS

- *The Rockets' arena has 18,300 seats for basketball.*
- *The arena has 103 luxury suites.*
- *As of 2008, the Rockets had retired five numbers—22 (Clyde Drexler), 23 (Calvin Murphy), 24 (Moses Malone), 34 (Hakeem Olajuwon), and 45 (Rudy Tomjanovich).*

The players and fans stand for the national anthem before a game in Houston's arena.

Dressed for Success

United States astronauts train in Houston. But that is not why the city's NBA team is called the Rockets. The story actually goes back to their days in San Diego.

When the team began playing in 1967, San Diego was known as the "City in Motion." At the time, nothing moved higher, faster, or farther than a rocket ship. Also, Atlas rockets were built in San Diego. These three factors led to the name *Rockets*. The team used a rocket in its **logo** in its early years and still uses one today. From 1972 to 1995, Houston's logo was an orange basketball surrounded by red streaks. They were meant to show the trail of a rocket in orbit.

The Rockets' team colors have changed over the years. In San Diego, the players wore green and gold uniforms. During the 1970s and 1980s, Houston's main colors were red, white, and yellow. Starting in the mid-1990s, the team wore dark blue and red pinstriped uniforms. In 2003, the Rockets returned to red and white.

High-scoring forward Stu Lantz models the team's green and gold colors from the 1960s.

UNIFORM BASICS

The basketball uniform is very simple. It consists of a roomy top and baggy shorts.

- The top hangs from the shoulders, with big "scoops" for the arms and neck. This style has not changed much over the years.

- Shorts, however, have changed a lot. They used to be very short, so players could move their legs freely. In the last 20 years, shorts have actually gotten longer and much baggier.

Basketball uniforms look the same as they did long ago ... until you look very closely. In the old days, the shorts had belts and buckles. The tops were made of a thick cotton called "jersey," which got very heavy when players sweated. Later, uniforms were made of shiny *satin*. They may have looked great, but they did not "breathe." Players got very hot! Today, most uniforms are made of *synthetic* materials that soak up sweat and keep the body cool.

Rafer Alston brings the ball up the court in the team's 2007–08 home uniform.

We Won!

The Rockets reached the NBA Finals twice in the 1980s and twice more in the 1990s. In 1980–81, Houston moved from the **Eastern Conference** to the Western Conference. Instead of competing against teams such as the Boston Celtics and Philadelphia 76ers, the Rockets regularly squared off against the Los Angeles Lakers. In fact, they met the Lakers in the first round of the 1981 playoffs. Moses Malone outplayed **All-Star** Kareem Abdul-Jabbar, and Houston won the series. The Rockets were unstoppable until they ran into the Celtics in the NBA Finals. Houston lost in six games.

Houston beat the Lakers in the playoffs again in 1985–86. Ralph Sampson hit an amazing shot at the buzzer in Game 5 to send Houston back to the NBA Finals. Once again, the Celtics had too much talent. They beat the Rockets in six games.

Houston's luck changed in the 1990s. In 1993–94, the Rockets set a record by winning their first 15 games. Hakeem Olajuwon—a young star on the 1986 team—was now a wise NBA **veteran**. He won the MVP award and was named **Defensive Player of the Year**. The Rockets finished atop the **Midwest Division** with 58 victories.

The Rockets met the Phoenix Suns in the second round of the playoffs that year. Houston blew an 18-point lead in Game 1 and a 20-point lead in Game 2. Things looked bad in Game 3 until fiery guard Vernon Maxwell exploded for 31 points in the second half and led his team to victory. The Rockets won three of the next four games to take the series.

After beating the Utah Jazz in the next round, the Rockets faced the New York Knicks in the NBA Finals. Both teams treated their fans to many great moments. Olajuwon and Knicks center Patrick Ewing had amazing battles every game. Sam Cassell, a rookie guard for the

LEFT: Vernon Maxwell races past the Phoenix Suns for a layup during the 1994 playoffs.   **RIGHT**: Hakeem Olajuwon rises for a shot over Patrick Ewing of the New York Knicks.

Rockets, hit a long **3-point shot** to win a game. Olajuwon blocked a shot at the end of Game 6 that could have won the series for the Knicks. In Game 7, the Rockets seized control early and held on to win 90–84.

The Rockets began the next season with another long winning streak. However, the team believed it needed another scorer to repeat as champions. The Rockets traded for Clyde Drexler, who had played in Houston in high school and college. Drexler averaged more than 20 points a game for the Rockets and brought the fans to their feet with his famous dunks. Houston, however, did not improve in the **standings**.

As the playoffs neared, no one expected the Rockets to defend their title. They did not seem to have the same spirit as the year before. But something wonderful happened when the **postseason** began. Against the Jazz in the first round, the Rockets found themselves in trouble in the final game of the series. Utah held a 12-point lead in the second half, but Olajuwon took over and won the game for the Rockets.

Against the Suns in the second round, the Rockets fell behind three games to one. Once again, they made a furious **comeback**. Robert Horry led the team to victory in **overtime** in Game 5. Mario Elie made a 3-pointer with seven seconds left to win Game 7. Next, the Rockets beat the San Antonio Spurs in the Western Conference Finals. Olajuwon was amazing against David Robinson in a battle of superstar centers.

After so many close calls, the Rockets were ready for the Orlando Magic when the NBA Finals began. They played good defense against Orlando's star players, Shaquille O'Neal and Penny Hardaway. Olajuwon earned MVP honors again for the Rockets, but Cassell and Kenny Smith were also fantastic. Houston's four-game sweep and second championship was truly a team victory.

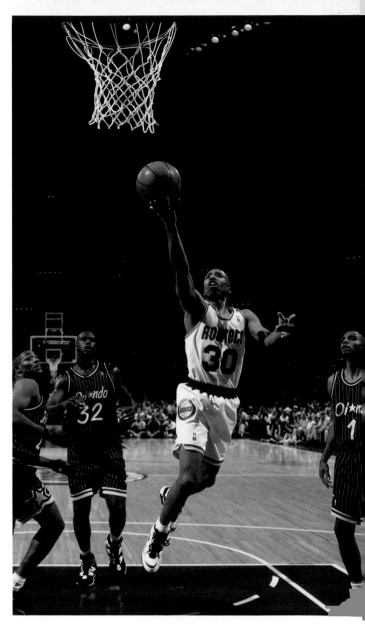

LEFT: Mario Elie celebrates during Houston's 1995 playoff run.
ABOVE: Kenny Smith scores a basket against the Orlando Magic.

Go-To Guys

To be a true star in the NBA, you need more than a great shot. You have to be a "go-to guy"—someone teammates trust to make the winning play when the seconds are ticking away in a big game. Rockets fans have had a lot to cheer about over the years, including these great stars …

THE PIONEERS

ELVIN HAYES   6´9˝ Forward/Center

- BORN: 11/17/1945
- PLAYED FOR TEAM: 1968–69 TO 1971–72 & 1981–82 TO 1983–84

Elvin Hayes was a true power forward. He could score from anywhere on the court, but he could also fight for rebounds under the basket. The "Big E" was the Rockets' first superstar.

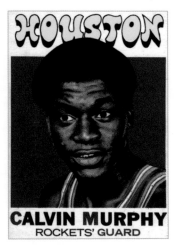

CALVIN MURPHY
ROCKETS' GUARD

CALVIN MURPHY   5´9˝ Guard

- BORN: 5/9/1948   • PLAYED FOR TEAM: 1970–71 TO 1982–83

Calvin Murphy averaged 30 points a game in college. But because of his small size, no one thought he would be a great player in the NBA. Murphy was that and more. He was the heart of the Rockets for 13 years and later entered the Basketball **Hall of Fame**.

MIKE NEWLIN

6´ 4˝ Guard

- BORN: 1/2/1949
- PLAYED FOR TEAM: 1971–72 TO 1978–79

Many Rockets had more talent than Mike Newlin, but no one had more heart. Newlin was tough and intelligent. When the Rockets needed to stop an opponent or make a basket, they could always count on him.

MOSES MALONE

6´ 10˝ Center

- BORN: 3/23/1955
- PLAYED FOR TEAM: 1976–77 TO 1981–82

Many fans thought Moses Malone had a "sixth sense" when it came to grabbing rebounds. Malone simply believed in out-working everyone else to get the ball. He led the Rockets in rebounds every year he was on the team and was the NBA MVP twice.

MIKE NEWLIN ▪ G

ROBERT REID

6´ 8˝ Forward

- BORN: 8/30/1955
- PLAYED FOR TEAM: 1977–78 TO 1987–88

Robert Reid was a key player for the Houston teams that won the Western Conference in 1981 and 1986. He was a good shooter, rebounder, passer, and defender. Whatever the team needed, Reid was ready and willing to give.

LEFT: Calvin Murphy   **ABOVE**: Mike Newlin

21

RALPH SAMPSON   7´ 4˝ Center

- BORN: 7/7/1960   • PLAYED FOR TEAM: 1983–84 TO 1987–88

No one had ever seen a player like Ralph Sampson. He could handle the ball like a guard and shoot like a forward, yet he was six inches taller

than many of the centers he played against. Some said Sampson could have been the greatest player ever, but knee injuries prevented him from reaching his full *potential*.

HAKEEM OLAJUWON   7´ 0˝ Center

- BORN: 1/21/1963
- PLAYED FOR TEAM: 1984–85 TO 2000–01

Hakeem "The Dream" Olajuwon did not pick up a basketball until he was a teenager. He worked hard to learn the game and quickly became a star. Olajuwon played with a hunger for victory that only a handful of leaders have ever brought to the court. He was the league MVP once and MVP of the NBA Finals twice.

CUTTINO MOBLEY   6´ 4˝ Guard

- BORN: 9/1/1975   • PLAYED FOR TEAM: 1998–99 TO 2003–04

Every team needs a player who can calmly make outside shots. For many years, Cuttino Mobley was the man the Rockets counted on to do this job—and more. Mobley was a good team player who was as tough on defense as he was with the ball in his hands.

ABOVE: Hakeem Olajuwon and Ralph Sampson
RIGHT: Tracy McGrady and Yao Ming

STEVE FRANCIS   6´ 3˝ Guard

• BORN: 2/21/1977   • PLAYED FOR TEAM: 1999–00 TO 2003–04 & 2008–09

Steve Francis was one of the NBA's most exciting players from the first day he pulled on a Houston jersey. Francis was the team's top scorer in three of his first four seasons and made the All-Star team three times. He loved to shoot with the game on the line.

YAO MING   7´ 6˝ Center

• BORN: 9/12/1980

• FIRST SEASON WITH TEAM: 2002–03

When Yao Ming first came to the NBA, some said he was too nice to be a superstar. Yao proved you can play hard, physical basketball on the court and still be a good guy off it. Yao had a great season in 2007–08 when he averaged 22 points, 11 rebounds, and two blocks.

TRACY McGRADY   6´ 8˝ Guard

• BORN: 5/24/1979

• FIRST SEASON WITH TEAM: 2004–05

The Rockets searched high and low for a superstar to pair with Yao Ming. They found their man in Tracy McGrady. He joined the NBA as a teenager and quickly proved that he was one of the most talented players in the league. McGrady led the Rockets to the playoffs in three of his first four seasons with the team.

On the Sidelines

The Rockets have had many good coaches over the years, starting with their first two, Jack McMahon and Alex Hannum. McMahon led the Rockets to the playoffs in just their second season. Hannum had guided three other teams to league championships.

The Rockets became a top NBA team under Tom Nissalke. Early in the 1976–77 season, Nissalke urged Houston to trade for Moses Malone. The Rockets sent two first-round draft choices to the Buffalo Braves. Malone quickly became one of the best players in the league.

During the 1980s, Del Harris and Bill Fitch led the Rockets to the NBA Finals. Both coaches were known for getting the most out of their players. Harris did it by being a "nice guy." Fitch was one of the toughest coaches in history.

From 1992 to 2003, the Rockets were coached by their former star, Rudy Tomjanovich. He built Houston's first championship team around Hakeem Olajuwon. Tomjanovich surrounded Olajuwon with players who could fill supporting roles one day and then perform like All-Stars the next. "Rudy T" remains a beloved figure in Houston basketball.

Rudy Tomjanovich gives instructions to Sam Cassell during the 1994 NBA Finals.

One Great Day

When the Rockets gave Houston its first pro basketball championship in 1993–94, fans all over the city began wearing buttons that said, "Believe It!" A year later, however, there were few believers left in Houston. The team struggled at times during the 1994–95 season. Houston's players learned a tough lesson: Winning two championships in a row is one of the hardest things to do in professional sports.

The Rockets were tired, injured, and unhappy as the 1995 playoffs began. No one thought they had a chance. Amazingly, their second championship would be even sweeter than their first.

As the Rockets took their home court for Game 4 of the NBA Finals against the Orlando Magic, they had a chance to make history. Houston was one victory away from a four-game sweep. Already in the playoffs, the Rockets had overcome the top three teams in the NBA. Orlando, with 57 wins, had tied for the league's fourth-best record.

The Magic played hard and took a one-point lead at the beginning of the fourth quarter. Houston fans rose to their feet to urge their

Robert Horry and Hakeem Olajuwon team up to stop Shaquille O'Neal during the 1995 NBA Finals.

players on. The Rockets responded with a spirited run. Mario Elie scored eight points to spark the offense. Hakeem Olajuwon shut down Shaquille O'Neal. With less than six minutes left, the Magic were desperate to stay close. Robert Horry nailed a long 3-pointer to end any hope of an Orlando comeback. The Rockets finished off the Magic, 113–101.

"To win the first time is a very *unique* feeling," remembers Olajuwon. "To win a second time is a different kind of thrill. You know the reward and that makes you want it even more."

Legend Has It

Did Hakeem Olajuwon make the greatest block in NBA history?

LEGEND HAS IT that he did. In Game 6 of the 1994 NBA Finals, the Rockets needed to win to stay alive. The New York Knicks had the ball as the clock wound down. Houston had trailed for much of the game, but now they held an 86–84 lead. New York set up a play for John Starks to shoot a 3-pointer. When Olajuwon saw what was happening, he darted around two Knicks and jumped as high as he could just as Starks released the ball. Olajuwon tipped the ball—and then avoided smashing into Starks and being whistled for a foul. The block saved the day for the Rockets. They celebrated by beating the Knicks for the title in Game 7.

Which Rocket wore different uniform numbers at home and on the road?

LEGEND HAS IT that Rick Barry did. Barry had always worn number 24. When he joined the Rockets in 1978, Moses Malone already had that number. Barry asked the NBA for special permission to wear number 2 at home and number 4 on the road. The league told Barry it was okay. It was the first time a player had ever been allowed to do this.

Rick Barry
FORWARD
ROCKETS

Which NBA coach built a doghouse in his team's dressing room?

LEGEND HAS IT that Bill Fitch did. In 1986, Fitch set up a red doghouse in the locker room. When a player did something wrong, Fitch would take a doll with the player's uniform number and place it in the house for all the players to see. "If they found their doll in the doghouse that meant they were in it, and they had better come talk it over with me," Fitch explained.

LEFT: Hakeem Olajuwon makes his famous block.
ABOVE: A trading card shows Rick Barry in his #4 jersey.

It Really Happened

Winning streaks are amazing things. For a team to go game after game without losing, a lot of different things must happen. A team must have good players, a smart coach, and play unselfish basketball. Its schedule must be "kind"—with the games spread out so everyone has a chance to rest. And it helps if a lot of games are at home, where the crowd can cheer the team to victory. A winning streak also takes a lot of luck. A team's players must be healthy and at their best.

That is what made the Rockets' winning streak in 2007–08 so fantastic. The team played 22 games before it finally lost. The last 10 victories came without Yao Ming. That meant it was up to team leaders Tracy McGrady and Shane Battier to get the job done. They did just that, and the rest of the Rockets also stepped up with great performances. Tired and sore, the Rockets kept winning and winning.

The streak finally ended at home against the Boston Celtics on March 18. Even though the Rockets lost by 20 points, the crowd stood and cheered. The scoreboard read: "Where 22 in a row happens." Houston's streak was the second-longest in NBA history.

Tracy McGrady gets a hug from Dikembe Mutombo during Houston's amazing 22-game winning streak.

The players were incredibly proud of what they accomplished. "Our names will be mentioned there with Hall of Fame people," Rafer Alston said. "We have something to tell our kids."

"When I'm old and gray and can't dribble this basketball anymore, I think I'll appreciate it," joked Battier.

McGrady hoped the streak would last forever but knew it wouldn't. "All good things must come to an end," he said with a smile.

Team Spirit

There is never a dull moment in the Rockets' arena. When the action on the court stops, fans get to see the Rocket Power Dancers, the acrobatic Launch Crew cheerleaders, and the G-Force Step Team. Meanwhile Clutch the Bear, Houston's **mascot**, works his way through the crowd.

One of the noisiest parts of the Rockets' arena is the section where the Red Rowdies sit. The Red Rowdies are a group of super-fans that began making themselves heard in 2006. Since then they have become famous throughout the NBA.

The Red Rowdies push team spirit to the limit. Their celebrations begin long before game time. They gather at one of the entrances and pump up Rockets fans as they enter the arena. During games, the Red Rowdies are sometimes as entertaining as the Rockets.

To become a member of the Red Rowdies, fans must **audition**. Of course, the judges include Houston players. And why not? They have to listen to the Red Rowdies all season long!

For Houston fans, the color red means go. They love their Rockets.

Timeline

The basketball season is played from October through June. That means each season takes place at the end of one year and the beginning of the next. In this timeline, the accomplishments of the Rockets are shown by season.

1967–68
The Rockets play their first season in San Diego.

1979–80
Rick Barry is the NBA's top free-throw shooter.

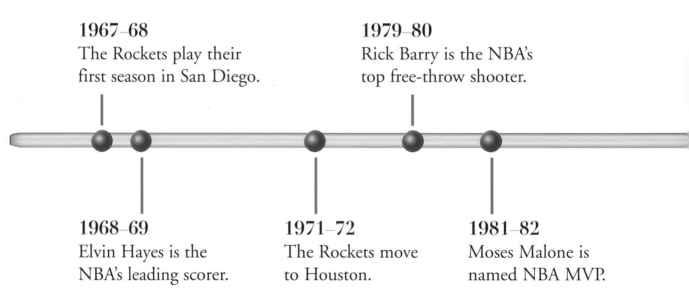

1968–69
Elvin Hayes is the NBA's leading scorer.

1971–72
The Rockets move to Houston.

1981–82
Moses Malone is named NBA MVP.

Art Williams drives to the basket for the Rockets during their first season.

Robert Reid, a star for the 1985–86 team.

 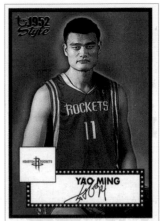

Yao Ming

1985–86
The Rockets reach the NBA Finals for the second time.

1999–00
Steve Francis is named co-**Rookie of the Year**.

2002–03
Yao Ming joins the Rockets.

1990–91
Don Chaney is named NBA **Coach of the Year**.

1994–95
The Rockets win the NBA Championship for the second year in a row.

2007–08
The Rockets win 22 games in a row.

Robert Horry celebrates Houston's second title.

Luis Scola, a key player on the 2007–08 team.

Fun Facts

TWIST AND SHOUT

Hakeem Olajuwon could do amazing things with his body. His ability to turn and twist without losing his balance made him a great offensive star. Olajuwon learned his moves growing up in Nigeria playing a sport called team handball.

NAME GAME

In 1967, pro basketball fans were amazed to hear that they could root for two teams with the same name. The NBA's newest team was the San Diego Rockets. The ABA had a team in Denver named the Rockets, too. They later became the Nuggets.

HOME COOKIN'

During the 1985–86 season, the Rockets won 20 games in a row at home. They went on to reach the NBA Finals that year.

LONG STORY SHORT

When Rudy Tomjanovich joined the Rockets, the team had a problem. His name was too long to squeeze onto his uniform. The Rockets decided to make it simple. They sewed *RUDY T* onto the back of his jersey.

HOT PANTS

During their first year in Houston, the Rockets used a logo that showed a basketball player with a flaming rocket strapped to his back.

RUDY TOMJANOVICH ▪ F

RISE AND SHINE

After the 2008 **Olympics** in Beijing, the Chinese government held a sports auction. One of the most popular items was the enormous bed built especially for Yao Ming.

LEFT: Hakeem Olajuwon twists in the air for a jump shot.
ABOVE: Rudy Tomjanovich, who was also known as "Rudy T."

Talking Hoops

"It's not up to anyone else to make me give my best."

—Hakeem Olajuwon, on what motivated him to be a great player

"Sport is the best means of communication between people from different religions and countries."

—Yao Ming, on what basketball means to him

"Yao is one great dude. Not cocky. Modest. Loving. Always hugging you. Always wanting to learn."

—Cuttino Mobley, on Yao Ming

"When you talk about the greatest players ever, Hakeem Olajuwon has to be very high on the list. Who else can play the game like he does?"

—Clyde Drexler, on his amazing teammate

"Never **underestimate** the heart of a champion."

—Rudy Tomjanovich, on what it takes to win it all

ABOVE: Yao Ming and Cuttino Mobley
RIGHT: Kenny Smith

"A professional athlete carries a lot of responsibility ... being responsible for my teammates, my team, and even the city I'm playing in."

—Kenny Smith, on the connection between a player and his team

"Blame is the coward's way out."

—Elvin Hayes, on a champion's attitude

"You've got to get the ball before you can shoot it."

—Moses Malone, on the importance of offensive rebounds

"I think of myself as the pioneer of the little guy. "

—Calvin Murphy, on what his rise to stardom meant to him

For the Record

The great Rockets teams and players have left their marks on the record books. These are the "best of the best" …

Ralph Sampson

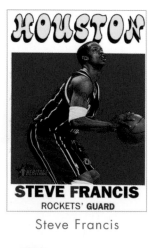

Steve Francis

ROCKETS AWARD WINNERS

WINNER	AWARD	SEASON
Tom Nissalke	Coach of the Year	1976–77
Moses Malone	Most Valuable Player	1978–79
Moses Malone	Most Valuable Player	1981–82
Ralph Sampson	Rookie of the Year	1983–84
Ralph Sampson	All-Star Game MVP	1984–85
Don Chaney	Coach of the Year	1990–91
Hakeem Olajuwon	Defensive Player of the Year	1992–93
Hakeem Olajuwon	Defensive Player of the Year	1993–94
Hakeem Olajuwon	Most Valuable Player	1993–94
Hakeem Olajuwon	NBA Finals MVP	1993–94
Hakeem Olajuwon	NBA Finals MVP	1994–95
Steve Francis	co-Rookie of the Year	1999–00

Sam Cassell, a star for the champs in 1993–94 and 1994–95.

ROCKETS ACHIEVEMENTS

ACHIEVEMENT	SEASON
Central Division Champions	1976–77
Western Conference Champions	1980–81
Midwest Division Champions	1985–86
Western Conference Champions	1985–86
Midwest Division Champions	1992–93
Midwest Division Champions	1993–94
Western Conference Champions	1993–94
NBA Champions	1993–94
Western Conference Champions	1994–95
NBA Champions	1994–95

1994 AND 1995 BACK-TO-BACK NBA CHAMPION
HOUSTON ROCKETS
1995-96 MEDIA GUIDE

RIGHT: Hakeem Olajuwon and Clyde Drexler show off Houston's championship trophies.　　**BELOW**: Two-time MVP Moses Malone

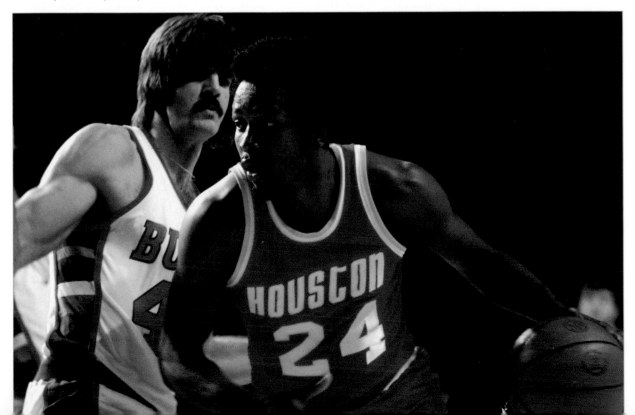

Pinpoints

The history of a basketball team is made up of many smaller stories. These stories take place all over the map—not just in the city a team calls "home." Match the push-pins on these maps to the Team Facts and you will begin to see the story of the Rockets unfold!

TEAM FACTS

1 Houston, Texas—*The Rockets have played here since 1971–72.*

2 San Diego, California—*The team played here from 1967–68 to 1970–71.*

3 Rayville, Louisiana—*Elvin Hayes was born here.*

4 Hamtramck, Michigan—*Rudy Tomjanovich was born here.*

5 Norwalk, Connecticut—*Calvin Murphy was born here.*

6 New York, New York—*Mario Elie was born here.*

7 Silver Spring, Maryland—*Steve Francis was born here.*

8 Petersburg, Virginia—*Moses Malone was born here.*

9 Andalusia, Alabama—*Robert Horry was born here.*

10 Bartow, Florida—*Tracy McGrady was born here.*

11 Lagos, Nigeria—*Hakeem Olajuwon was born here.*

12 Shanghai, China—*Yao Ming was born here.*

Robert Horry

43

Play Ball

Basketball is a sport played by two teams of five players. NBA games have four 12-minute quarters—48 minutes in all—and the team that scores the most points when time has run out is the winner. Most baskets count for two points. Players who make shots from beyond the three-point line receive an extra point. Baskets made from the free-throw line count for one point. Free throws are penalty shots awarded to a team, usually after an opponent has committed a foul. A foul is called when one player makes hard contact with another.

Players can move around all they want, but the player with the ball cannot. He must bounce the ball with one hand or the other (but never both) in order to go from one part of the court to another. As long as he keeps "dribbling," he can keep moving.

In the NBA, teams must attempt a shot every 24 seconds, so there is little time to waste. The job of the defense is to make it as difficult as possible to take a good shot—and to grab the ball if the other team shoots and misses.

This may sound simple, but anyone who has played the game knows that basketball can be very complicated. Every player on the court has a job to do. Different players have different strengths and weaknesses. The coach must mix these players in just the right way, and teach them to work together as one.

The more you play and watch basketball, the more "little things" you are likely to notice. The next time you are at a game, look for these plays:

PLAY LIST

ALLEY-OOP—A play where the passer throws the ball just to the side of the rim—so a teammate can catch it and dunk in one motion.

BACK-DOOR PLAY—A play where the passer waits for his teammate to fake the defender away from the basket—then throws him the ball when he cuts back toward the basket.

KICK-OUT—A play where the ball-handler waits for the defense to surround him—then quickly passes to a teammate who is open for an outside shot. The ball is not really kicked in this play; the term comes from the action of pinball machines.

NO-LOOK PASS—A play where the passer fools a defender (with his eyes) into covering one teammate—then suddenly passes to another without looking.

PICK-AND-ROLL—A play where one teammate blocks or "picks off" another's defender with his body—then cuts to the basket for a pass in the confusion.

Glossary

BASKETBALL WORDS TO KNOW

3-POINT SHOT—A basket made from behind the 3-point line.

ALL-STAR—A player selected to play in the annual All-Star Game.

AMERICAN BASKETBALL ASSOCIATION (ABA)—The basketball league that played for nine seasons starting in 1967. Prior to the 1976–77 season, four ABA teams joined the NBA, and the rest went out of business.

CENTRAL DIVISION—A group of teams that plays in the central part of the country.

COACH OF THE YEAR—An award given each season to the league's best coach.

DEFENSIVE PLAYER OF THE YEAR—The award given each year to the league's best defensive player.

DRAFT PICK—A college player selected or "drafted" by NBA teams each summer.

EASTERN CONFERENCE—A group of teams split up into smaller groups that play in the East. The winner of the Eastern Conference meets the winner of the Western Conference in the league finals.

HALL OF FAME—The museum in Springfield, Massachusetts, where basketball's greatest players are honored. A player voted into the Hall of Fame is sometimes called a "Hall of Famer."

LINEUP—The list of players who are playing in a game.

MIDWEST DIVISION—A group of teams that plays in the central part of the country.

MOST VALUABLE PLAYER (MVP)—The award given each year to the league's best player; also given to the best player in the league finals and All-Star Game.

NATIONAL BASKETBALL ASSOCIATION (NBA)—The professional league that has been operating since 1946–47.

NBA DRAFT—The annual meeting where teams pick from a group of the best college players.

NBA FINALS—The playoff series that decides the champion of the league.

OVERTIME—The extra period played when a game is tied after 48 minutes.

PLAYOFFS—The games played after the season to determine the league champion.

POSTSEASON—Another term for playoffs.

PROFESSIONAL—A player or team that plays a sport for money. College players are not paid, so they are considered "amateurs."

ROLE PLAYERS—People who are asked to do specific things when they are in a game.

ROOKIE—A player in his first season.

ROOKIE OF THE YEAR—The annual award given to the league's best first-year player.

STANDINGS—A daily list of teams, starting with the team with the best record and ending with the team with the worst record.

SUBSTITUTES—Players who begin most games on the bench.

VETERAN—A player with great experience.

WESTERN CONFERENCE FINALS—The playoff series that determines which team from the West will play the best team in the East for the NBA Championship.

OTHER WORDS TO KNOW

AGILE—Quick and graceful.

AUDITION—Try out.

CENTURY—A period of 100 years.

COMEBACK—The process of catching up from behind, or making up a large deficit.

CONTENDERS—People who compete for a championship.

DEFUNCT—No longer existing.

FORMULA—A set way of doing something.

INVESTORS—People who spend their money for the purpose of making more money.

LOGO—A symbol or design that represents a company or team.

MASCOT—An animal or person believed to bring a group good luck.

OLYMPICS—An international sports competition held every four years.

POTENTIAL—Capable of becoming better.

SATIN—A smooth, shiny fabric.

SYNTHETIC—Made in a laboratory, not in nature.

UNDERESTIMATE—Place too low a value on.

UNIQUE—Special or one of a kind.

Places to Go

ON THE ROAD

HOUSTON ROCKETS
1510 Polk Street
Houston, Texas 77002
(713) 758-7200

NAISMITH MEMORIAL BASKETBALL HALL OF FAME
1000 West Columbus Avenue
Springfield, Massachusetts 01105
(877) 4HOOPLA

ON THE WEB

THE NATIONAL BASKETBALL ASSOCIATION www.nba.com
  • *Learn more about the league's teams, players, and history*

THE HOUSTON ROCKETS www.nba.com/rockets
  • *Learn more about the Rockets*

THE BASKETBALL HALL OF FAME www.hoophall.com
  • *Learn more about history's greatest players*

ON THE BOOKSHELF

To learn more about the sport of basketball, look for these books at your library or bookstore:

  • Hareas, John. *Basketball*. New York, New York: DK, 2005.

  • Hughes, Morgan. *Basketball*. Vero Beach, Florida: Rourke Publishing, 2005.

  • Thomas, Keltie. *How Basketball Works*. Berkeley, California: Maple Tree Press, distributed through Publishers Group West, 2005.

Index

PAGE NUMBERS IN **BOLD** REFER TO ILLUSTRATIONS.

Abdul-Jabbar, Kareem 16

Alston, Rafer **15**, 31

Barkley, Charles 9

Barry, Rick 29, **29**, 34

Battier, Shane **4**, 30, 31

Block, John 6

Cassell, Sam 7, 17, 19, **24**, **40**

Chaney, Don 35, 40

Drexler, Clyde 9, **9**, 13, 18, 38, **41**

Elie, Mario **18**, 19, 27, 43

Ewing, Patrick 17, **17**

Fitch, Bill 25, 29

Francis, Steve 23, 35, 40, **40**, 43

Gambee, Dave 6

Hannum, Alex 25

Hardaway, Penny 19

Harris, Del 25

Hayes, Elvin 6, **6**, 20, 34, 39, 43

Horry, Robert 9, 19, 27, **27**, **35**, 43, **43**

Kojis, Don 6

Lantz, Stu **14**

Malone, Moses 7, **7**, 13, 16, 21, 25, 29, 34, 39, 40, **41**, 43

Maxwell, Vernon 9, **16**, 17

McGrady, Tracy **10**, 11, 23, **23**, 30, 31, **31**, 43

McMahon, Jack 25

Mobley, Cuttino 22, 38, **38**

Murphy, Calvin 7, 13, 20, **20**, 39, 43

Mutombo, Dikembe **31**

Nissalke, Tom 25, 40

Newlin, Mike 7, 21, **21**

Olajuwon, Hakeem 7, **8**, 9, 13, 17, **17**, 18, 19, 22, **22**, 25, 27, **27**, 28, **28**, 36, **36**, 38, 40, **41**, 43

O'Neal, Shaquille 9, 19, 27, **27**

Reid, Robert 21, **35**

Riley, Pat 6

Robinson, David 19

Sampson, Ralph 7, 16, 22, **22**, 40, **40**

Scola, Luis **35**

Smith, Kenny 7, 19, **19**, 39, **39**

Starks, John 28, **28**

Thorpe, Otis 9

Tomjanovich, Rudy 7, 9, 13, **24**, 25, 37, **37**, 38, 43

Williams, Art **34**

Yao, Ming **4**, **10**, 11, 23, **23**, 30, 35, **35**, 37, 38, **38**, 43

The Team

MARK STEWART has written more than 20 books on basketball, and over 100 sports books for kids. He grew up in New York City during the 1960s rooting for the Knicks and Nets, and now takes his two daughters, Mariah and Rachel, to watch them play. Mark comes from a family of writers. His grandfather was Sunday Editor of *The New York Times* and his mother was Articles Editor of *The Ladies Home Journal* and *McCall's*. Mark has profiled hundreds of athletes over the last 20 years. He has also written several books about his native New York, and New Jersey, his home today. Mark is a graduate of Duke University, with a degree in history. He lives with his daughters and wife, Sarah, overlooking Sandy Hook, New Jersey.

MATT ZEYSING is the resident historian at the Basketball Hall of Fame in Springfield, Massachusetts. His research interests include the origins of the game of basketball, the development of professional basketball in the first half of the twentieth century, and the culture and meaning of basketball in American society.